The woman of enneagram 2

Enneagram For Women, Volume 2

Maria Rondon

Published by Maria Rondon, 2024.

MARIA RONDON
THE WOMAN OF ENNEAGRAM
2
LOVE, MARRIAGE AND SUCCESS EDITION

ENNEAGRAM 2 FOR WOMEN.

Sans Serif Agency Web Site: http://www.sansserifagency.com
Sans Serif Agency is a trademark of Sans Serif Agency.
Library of Congress Cataloging-in-Publication Data:
Rondon, Maria.
Enneagram 2 for women / Maria Rondon. — 1st ed.

CONTENT
Understanding Yourself: A Guide for Enneagram Twos

- The Enneagram and the Power of Self-Discovery: A historical overview of the Enneagram and its relevance to self-knowledge, specifically for Enneagram Twos.

- The Two's Journey: Embracing Your Strengths and Working with Your Challenges: How self-understanding can empower Type Two women in various aspects of their lives, including relationships, career, and personal growth.

Chapter 1: Building Deep Connections

- The Art of Healthy Relationships for Twos: Strategies for understanding and appreciating Enneagram type differences when navigating relationships. (Consider including a section on "Love Languages" here)
- The Two's Guide to Healthy Boundaries: Techniques for setting healthy boundaries while maintaining strong

connections.

- Subtype Spotlight: How Self-Preservation, Social, and Sexual Twos Approach Relationships: Analyzing how subtypes influence how Twos connect with others.

Chapter 2: Finding Balance and Fulfillment

- From People-Pleasing to Purpose: Strategies for maintaining a healthy balance between personal needs and professional goals.
- Creating Your Support System: The importance of building and maintaining supportive relationships at work and beyond.

Chapter 3: Cultivating Self-Love and Growth

- Beyond the Need to Be Needed: Techniques and exercises to overcome the potential challenge of codependency and unhealthy helping patterns.
- The Power of Authenticity: Developing a strong sense of self-worth and personal boundaries.

Chapter 4: Nurturing Your Wellbeing

- Nourishing Body and Mind: Exploring how mindful eating habits and self-care practices can support physical and emotional wellbeing for Twos.
- The Power of Connection and Movement: Discussing different forms of physical activity and social connection that can benefit Twos in managing stress and promoting well-being.

Chapter 5: Supportive Parenting

- Raising Confident Children: Moving Beyond Perfectionism: Strategies for balancing expectations and fostering a positive learning environment for your children.
- The Gift of Presence: Techniques for being present and consciously involved in parenting while also taking care of yourself.

Chapter 6: Exploring Your Spiritual Path

- The Enneagram and Your Deepest Longing: Exploring how the Enneagram can be a tool for deepening spiritual connection for Twos.
- Spiritual Practices for Nurturing the Soul: Incorporating a variety of spiritual practices that may resonate with different readers, such as meditation, nature connection, or service to others.

Chapter 7: Growth and Integration

- Your Wings: Understanding the Influences of Type Three and Type One: A section dedicated to exploring how the wings (Type 2w3 and Type 2w1) influence personality, preferences, and challenges of Twos.
- Growth and Integration: Moving Towards Health: Examining how Twos integrate towards Type Four (in growth) and disintegrate towards Type Eight (under stress), and offering strategies for managing these movements.
- Enneagram Twos in Action

CHAPTER 8: 21 DAYS WORKBOOK

Understanding Yourself: A Guide for Enneagram Twos

the Enneagram is widely used not only for self-knowledge but also in fields such as counseling, business, education, and spiritual development. Its value lies in its ability to provide deep insights into the human psyche, fostering greater self-awareness, empathy, and compassion for others. At its core, the Enneagram serves as a guide for individuals to recognize their inherent strengths, blind spots, and defense mechanisms. By understanding one's Enneagram type and the unconscious patterns driving behavior, people can embark on a journey of transformation, shedding dysfunctional habits and aligning more fully with their highest potential. The enduring relevance of the Enneagram stems from its capacity to reveal the universal aspects of human nature while honoring the uniqueness of each individual's experiences. As an integrative system, it offers a holistic framework for personal growth, interpersonal relationships, and ultimately, the realization of our true, authentic selves.

"The Enneagram and the Power of Self-Discovery: A Historical Overview and Its Relevance to Self-Knowledge, Specifically for Enneagram Twos"

For Enneagram Type Two women, known as The Helpers or Givers, the journey of self-discovery through the Enneagram opens up profound avenues for understanding themselves, their motivations, and how they relate to others. Type Twos are characterized by their desire to be loved, appreciated, and needed, often putting the needs of others before their own. The Enneagram, with its rich historical background and psychological depth, offers Type Twos a mirror to reflect on their innermost desires and fears, guiding them towards greater self-knowledge and fulfillment.

The Enneagram as a Tool for Self-Discovery for Type 2s

The historical origins of the Enneagram, tracing back to ancient wisdom traditions, imbue it with a timeless relevance that resonates deeply with the quest for understanding human nature. For Type Two women, this quest often centers around their relationships with others and their role as nurturers and caregivers. The Enneagram's nuanced approach to personality types sheds light on the strengths and challenges inherent in the Type Two personality, offering a path to balance, self-care, and ultimately, self-love.

Understanding the Motivations of Type 2s

At the heart of the Type Two personality is the belief that being loved and valued is contingent upon their ability to meet the needs of others. This belief can lead to patterns of over-giving, seeking validation through acts of service, and neglecting their own needs. The Enneagram provides insight into these patterns, helping Type Twos recognize the difference between genuine altruism and the compulsion to help as a means of securing love and approval.

The Power of Awareness and Acceptance

For Type Twos, the journey of self-discovery facilitated by the Enneagram is both challenging and liberating. It requires confronting deeply ingrained beliefs about self-worth and dependency on others for validation. However, through increased awareness and acceptance of their true selves, Type Twos can begin to cultivate a healthier relationship with themselves and others. They can learn to set boundaries, express their needs, and recognize the value of self-care.

Expanding the Capacity for Empathy and Compassion

The Enneagram not only fosters self-understanding but also enhances empathy and compassion for others. By understanding the motivations and fears that drive not only themselves but also those around them, Type Twos can deepen their connections with others in more authentic and meaningful ways. This expanded capacity for empathy enriches their relationships and broadens their understanding of the human experience.

Embracing the Journey of Growth

The path of self-discovery for Enneagram Type Two women is an ongoing journey of growth, self-acceptance, and transformation. By engaging with the Enneagram as a tool for self-knowledge, Type Twos can navigate the complexities of their personality with greater insight and clarity. This journey empowers them to embrace their inherent worth, cultivate genuine self-love, and live more authentically, fulfilling their true potential while continuing to enrich the lives of others with their innate gifts of compassion and care.

In exploring the Enneagram and its relevance to self-knowledge, Type Two women are invited to embark on a transformative journey.

This journey promises not only a deeper understanding of themselves and their place in the world but also a greater capacity for love, connection, and spiritual transcendence.

"The Two's Journey: Embracing Your Strengths and Working with Your Challenges"

For Enneagram Type Two women, known for their warmth, generosity, and inherent desire to be loved and needed, the journey towards self-understanding is both illuminating and essential. The Enneagram serves as a mirror, reflecting both the beauty of their giving nature and the pitfalls of their fear of unworthiness. Understanding oneself as a Type Two opens the door to balancing these aspects, enabling women of this type to navigate their relationships, careers, and personal growth with greater awareness and authenticity.

Embracing Your Strengths

Type Two women possess a unique set of strengths that, when recognized and embraced, can lead to profound fulfillment and impact. Their natural empathy and intuition in understanding others' needs make them exceptional friends, partners, and colleagues. Twos have an innate ability to nurture and support, creating environments where love and care flourish. In the workplace, their collaborative spirit and willingness to assist are invaluable, often becoming the glue that holds teams together.

However, the true power of Type Two's strengths lies in their capacity for unconditional love and compassion, not just for others but, importantly, for themselves. Recognizing that their worth is inherent and not contingent on their service to others marks the beginning of a transformative journey towards self-acceptance and empowerment.

Working with Your Challenges

The path of growth for Type Two women involves confronting and working with their challenges, particularly their tendency to prioritize others' needs over their own and their struggle with acknowledging their own needs and desires. This often stems from a deep-seated fear of being unlovable or unnecessary, leading to patterns of overgiving, possessiveness, or manipulative behavior in an unconscious attempt to secure love and appreciation.

Self-understanding empowers Type Two women to recognize these patterns and the motivations behind them, creating space for change. Setting boundaries, practicing self-care, and learning to express their needs assertively are crucial steps in this process. Moreover, exploring their own passions and interests independent of their relationships with others allows Type Twos to discover a sense of self-worth that is not tied to their role as helpers.

Navigating Relationships and Career

Armed with self-awareness, Type Two women can approach their relationships and careers with a new perspective. In personal relationships, understanding their tendencies allows for healthier dynamics, where love and care are given freely, without expectations or conditions. Professionally, acknowledging their value and contributions can lead to more fulfilling career paths that align with their true passions and talents, rather than merely where they feel needed.

The Power of Self-Discovery

The journey of self-discovery for Enneagram Type Two women is a path of balancing the beautiful aspects of their giving nature with the importance of self-care and assertiveness. By embracing their strengths and working with their challenges, Type Twos can find a deeper sense of fulfillment, independence, and authenticity in all areas of their lives. The Enneagram, with its rich history and insights into the human psyche, offers a roadmap for this journey, guiding Type Two women towards realizing their highest potential and embracing their true, authentic selves.

Chapter 1:
Building Deep Connections

1

The Art of Healthy Relationships for 2s: Strategies for Understanding and Appreciating Enneagram Type Differences When Navigating Relationships

For Enneagram Type 2 women, who are inherently focused on relationships and possess a deep desire to be loved and appreciated, understanding the complexities of interpersonal dynamics is crucial. The Enneagram offers a roadmap for Type 2s to not only navigate their relationships with greater awareness but also to appreciate the rich tapestry of personality types they interact with. Incorporating an understanding of "Love Languages" can further enhance this journey, providing practical strategies for connecting with loved ones in meaningful ways.

Embracing Enneagram Type Differences

Recognizing and appreciating the differences in Enneagram types is the first step toward building healthier, more fulfilling relationships.

Each type has its unique worldview, motivations, and coping mechanisms, which can significantly influence how individuals express love and desire to be loved in return. For Type 2s, developing an understanding of these differences is essential in fostering connections that are both supportive and reciprocal.

Strategies for embracing type differences include:

Educate Yourself: Learn about the nine Enneagram types, focusing on their core desires, fears, and key motivations. This knowledge can illuminate why people react and interact in certain ways, helping Type 2s to empathize with and support their loved ones more effectively.

Practice Active Listening: Make a conscious effort to listen to the needs and concerns of others without immediately trying to fix or nurture. Sometimes, simply being present and offering a listening ear is more valuable than any action you could take.

Communicate Openly: Share your own needs and experiences as a Type 2 with your loved ones. Open communication can demystify your actions and reactions, making it easier for others to understand and meet your needs.

Integrating Love Languages

The concept of "Love Languages" — words of affirmation, acts of service, receiving gifts, quality time, and physical touch — complements the Enneagram by offering a practical framework for expressing and receiving love. For Type 2 women, becoming fluent in these languages can enhance their relationships in several ways:

Discover Your Own Love Language: Understanding how you prefer to receive love can help you communicate your needs more clearly to others, reducing feelings of being unappreciated or misunderstood.

Learn the Love Languages of Your Loved Ones: By identifying and speaking the love languages of the people close to you, you can show your love in ways that resonate deeply with them, fostering a sense of connection and appreciation.

Adapt Your Approach: Recognize that your natural inclination to offer love through acts of service may not always align with the love language of the recipient. Being willing to adapt your approach can lead to more meaningful exchanges of affection and support.

For Enneagram Type 2 women, the journey toward building deep and meaningful connections is both a personal and relational endeavor. By leveraging the insights provided by the Enneagram and the practical applications of Love Languages, Type 2s can cultivate relationships that are not only nurturing for others but also fulfilling and sustaining for themselves. In doing so, they can move beyond the desire to be needed, embracing a more balanced and authentic way of relating that honors both their own needs and the uniqueness of those they love.

The 2s Guide to Healthy Boundaries: Techniques for Setting Healthy Boundaries While Maintaining Strong Connections

For Enneagram Type Two women, the desire to be loved, appreciated, and deemed indispensable often leads to a tendency to overextend themselves in their relationships. While their generosity and nurturing spirit are among their greatest strengths, without clear boundaries, Twos risk burnout and may feel unappreciated or taken for granted. Establishing healthy boundaries is crucial for Type Twos to maintain their wellbeing and sustain strong, balanced relationships.

Understanding the Importance of Boundaries

Boundaries are the limits we set around our time, energy, and emotions to protect our wellbeing and respect our needs and values. For Type Two women, setting boundaries can be challenging as it may feel counterintuitive to their instinct to always be available and helpful. However, boundaries are not barriers to connection but rather the foundation for more honest, respectful, and mutually supportive relationships.

Techniques for Setting Healthy Boundaries

Self-Reflection: Begin by identifying your limits. Understand what you can give without feeling depleted or resentful. Reflect on instances where you felt overwhelmed or taken advantage of, and consider what boundaries could have protected your energy.

Communicate Clearly: Express your needs and limits to others with clarity and kindness. Use "I" statements to convey your feelings and expectations without placing blame. For example, "I feel valued when we share responsibilities" instead of "You never help me."

Practice Saying No: Saying no is a powerful boundary-setting tool. Start small and practice in situations where the stakes are low. Remember, saying no to others often means saying yes to your needs and wellbeing.

Seek Balance in Giving and Receiving: Monitor your relationships for reciprocity. Healthy relationships involve a balance of give and take. If you find yourself always on the giving end, it may be time to reassess and communicate your needs for support and assistance.

Prioritize Self-Care: Setting boundaries is an act of self-care. Ensure you're allocating time for your interests, relaxation, and self-nurturing activities. This not only protects your energy but also models healthy behavior for those around you.

Reframe Boundary-Setting: Understand that setting boundaries is an act of kindness. It prevents resentment and burnout, allowing you to engage more fully and authentically in your relationships.

Embracing the Power of Self-Discovery

the journey of self-discovery offered by the Enneagram is not just about understanding their personality but also about learning how to navigate their relationships with grace and strength. By embracing the practice of setting healthy boundaries, Type Twos can cultivate relationships that honor their need to give and their right to receive, fostering deeper connections that nourish both themselves and their loved ones.

In doing so, Type Two women embody the true spirit of the Enneagram—a tool for growth, transformation, and the realization of our highest potential in both personal and interpersonal realms. Through self-knowledge and the application of these techniques, Type Twos can enjoy the full richness of their relationships, grounded in mutual respect, understanding, and genuine connection.

Subtype Spotlight: How Self-Preservation, Social, and Sexual 2s Approach Relationships

The Enneagram identifies three subtypes in each personality type, reflecting the primary instinctual drives: Self-Preservation, Social, and Sexual (One-to-One). For Type Two women, these subtypes color how they express their nurturing tendencies and seek connection and validation from others.

Self-Preservation 2s: "The Warmth Seeker"

Self-Preservation Twos are driven by a need for personal security and comfort, often focusing their nurturing energy on creating a stable and safe environment for themselves and their loved ones. Their approach to relationships is more practical, offering care through acts of service that enhance the physical well-being and comfort of those they love. They may struggle with directly asking for help, fearing that it undermines their self-sufficiency.

Strategies for Connection: For Self-Preservation Twos, building deep connections involves acknowledging their needs and learning to express them clearly. Emphasizing open communication about their desires and vulnerabilities can strengthen their relationships, allowing them to receive the support and care they so freely give to others.

Social 2s: "The Ambassadors"

Social 2s are outwardly focused on the needs of the community or group, often taking on roles that allow them to be at the center of social networks. They offer support and care by mobilizing resources, organizing events, or advocating for others. Their challenge lies in balancing their attention between the group's needs and their personal relationships, sometimes neglecting close connections for the sake of the wider community.

Strategies for Connection: For Social Twos, deepening personal relationships may require setting aside dedicated time for individual connections outside of their social roles. Prioritizing intimacy and one-on-one interactions can help them nurture their closest bonds without the distractions of their broader social responsibilities.

Sexual 2s: "The Companions"

Sexual 2s seek intimacy and connection through close, one-to-one relationships, often focusing their nurturing and supportive energy on specific individuals. They desire to be seen as irreplaceable by their partners or close friends, sometimes leading to intensity in their connections. The challenge for Sexual Twos is to avoid over-identifying with their relationships and to maintain a sense of independence and self-worth outside of them.

Strategies for Connection: For Sexual 2s, healthy relationships are built on mutual respect and independence. Cultivating interests and activities separate from their partners or close friends can enhance their sense of self and prevent relationship dynamics from becoming overly enmeshed.

The Shadow Side:

Each subtype has a potential "shadow" that emerges when their core needs are unmet. Here's a glimpse of how it might manifest:

Self-Preservation Twos: In their shadow, they might become overly controlling or resistant to change, fearing disruption to their comfort zone. They could struggle with expressing vulnerability, creating a sense of emotional distance in relationships.

Social Twos: When feeling unseen or excluded, Social Twos might resort to manipulation or people-pleasing behaviors to gain approval from the group. This can lead to inauthentic connections and a loss of self.

Sexual Twos: If their sense of security within a relationship feels threatened, Sexual Twos might become possessive or jealous. Their intensity can be overwhelming for partners, pushing them away.

Through the Eyes of Others:

Understanding how different Enneagram types perceive Two subtypes can foster better communication:

Self-Preservation Twos: Appreciative partners recognize their efforts to create a secure and comfortable environment. However, some might find their focus on practicality a turn-off, longing for more emotional expression.

Social Twos: Their enthusiasm and ability to connect people are valued. But, some might find their constant "on" persona exhausting and crave deeper, one-on-one interactions.

Sexual Twos: Their passionate nature is admired. However, partners might feel smothered by their intensity and need for constant reassurance.

Chapter 2:
Finding Balance and Fulfillment

Balancing Acts: Navigating Personal Needs and Professional Goals with Heart

In the relentless quest to please others and achieve professional milestones, Enneagram type 2 women often find themselves at a crossroads. They struggle to balance their generous tendencies with their own needs and aspirations. This chapter delves into the depths of this struggle, proposing strategies that not only promote self-awareness but also pave the way towards a healthier balance and a more fulfilling professional and personal life.

The Generosity Conundrum

Enneagram type 2 women are known for their warmth, generosity, and innate ability to tune into the needs of others. This tendency to prioritize others' well-being over their own, however, can lead to a cycle of self-neglect and resentment. The key to breaking this cycle is not to suppress the generous nature of the Type 2, but to redirect it: first towards oneself and then towards others in a more balanced manner.

Acknowledging Personal Needs

The first step towards balance is recognizing that having needs is not a sign of weakness but a fundamental aspect of the human condition. Type 2 women must learn to identify and value their own needs with the same intensity they perceive those of their partners, colleagues, or loved ones. This may require deep introspection and the development of a mindful self-observation practice to distinguish between the desire to please and genuine personal needs.

Establishing Healthy Boundaries

The ability to set clear boundaries is essential to protect personal and professional space. This does not mean building walls, but rather defining lines that allow Type 2 women to give generously without losing themselves in the process. Learning to say "no" is as important as knowing when to say "yes," and it is a skill that can be developed with practice and determination.

Reconnecting with Personal Purpose

Beyond professional expectations and the desire to please, lies each individual's unique personal purpose. Type 2 women can reconnect with their purpose by dedicating time to explore their passions, values, and what truly makes them feel alive. This exploration may lead to a reevaluation of professional goals, aligning them more closely with what they genuinely want to achieve in life.

The Balance of Giving and Receiving

At the core of a healthy balance lies the act of balancing giving with receiving. Type 2 women must learn to accept help, love, and support from others with the same grace they offer theirs. Recognizing that it is possible and necessary to receive allows for a more equitable flow of energy in all relationships, including professional ones.

The journey of Enneagram type 2 women from pleasing others to finding a healthy balance and a fulfilling life is both challenging and enriching. By adopting strategies that foster self-awareness, self-acceptance, and self-realization, they can successfully navigate between their personal needs and professional goals. This balance not only benefits them but also enriches the lives of those who have the privilege of knowing them.

Empowering the Giver: Practical Strategies for Enneagram Type 2 Women

Having explored the core challenges and underlying motivations of Enneagram type 2 women, let's delve into practical strategies that can empower them to navigate this balancing act.

Schedule Self-Care Rituals: Block time in your calendar for activities that nourish your mind, body, and spirit. This could be anything from a relaxing bath with essential oils to a mindful walk in nature, or indulging in a creative hobby. Treat these appointments with the same respect you would a client meeting.

Practice Saying "No" with Grace: Saying "no" doesn't diminish your kindness; it strengthens it. When faced with a request that drains your energy or disrupts your priorities, communicate your boundaries politely but firmly. Offer an alternative solution if possible, demonstrating your willingness to help while honoring your own needs.

Build a Support System: Surround yourself with individuals who appreciate you for who you are, not just for what you do. Cultivate friendships with people who are assertive and can gently remind you to prioritize yourself. A therapist specializing in the Enneagram can also be a valuable resource for deeper self-discovery and support.

Celebrate Small Wins: Acknowledge and celebrate your accomplishments, big or small. This reinforces a positive self-image and motivates you to continue on your journey towards balance.

Embrace Imperfection: Type 2s often strive for flawlessness in their caregiving and professional roles. Remember, everyone makes mistakes. Learn to forgive yourself and embrace a growth mindset, focusing on progress rather than perfection.

By incorporating these strategies into their daily lives, Enneagram type 2 women can move from self-sacrifice to self-care, fostering a deeper sense of fulfillment and enriching every aspect of their lives. They can become not just the givers, but also the thriving leaders and fulfilled individuals they were always meant to be.

Building Your Support System: The importance of constructing and maintaining supportive relationships in the workplace and beyond. In a world where work and personal demands often seem to exceed our capabilities, the importance of having a solid support system becomes increasingly evident, especially for Enneagram type 2 women. This section explores how building and maintaining supportive relationships is not only vital for the emotional and professional well-being of type 2 women, but also crucial for achieving lasting balance and fulfillment in all aspects of their lives.

The Supportive Nature of Type 2

Type 2 women are characterized by their empathy, generosity, and innate tendency to prioritize others' needs over their own. While these qualities make them exceptional friends and colleagues, they can also lead them to neglect building their own support network. Recognizing the need to receive, as well as to give support, is a critical step towards personal and professional development.

Fostering Authentic Relationships

The first step in creating a support system is nurturing authentic relationships both in the workplace and personal life. This involves seeking connections that are not only based on reciprocal help and assistance, but also on genuine exchange of experiences, aspirations, and vulnerabilities. For type 2 women, this may mean overcoming reluctance to express their own needs and accepting that interdependence is a strength, not a weakness.

Maintaining Supportive Relationships

Once established, these relationships require care and ongoing attention to thrive. For type 2 women, this means practicing open and honest communication, regularly dedicating time to connect with friends and colleagues, and showing appreciation for the support received. Equally important is the willingness to reassess and adjust relationship dynamics that no longer serve their emotional or professional well-being.

The Importance of Diversity in the Support System

An effective support system is diverse, composed of individuals who offer different perspectives, skills, and types of support. For type 2 women, this may include mentors who guide their professional development, friends who provide emotional comfort, and colleagues who inspire and challenge their ideas. This diversity ensures that, regardless of the situation, type 2 women will have someone to turn to.

For type 2 women, building and maintaining a solid support system is essential for finding balance and fulfillment. By focusing on authenticity, reciprocity, and diversity in their relationships, they can ensure a support network that not only sustains them in times of need but also celebrates with them in moments of success. This chapter underscores that by recognizing the importance of receiving support as much as giving it, type 2 women can move towards a more balanced and satisfying life, at work and beyond.

Chapter 3:
Cultivating Self-Love and Growth

Beyond the Need to Be Needed: Techniques and exercises to overcome the potential challenge of codependency and unhealthy helping patterns.

The path to self-love and personal growth for Enneagram type 2 women often involves facing and transforming the tendency towards codependency and unhealthy helping. This section delves into techniques and exercises designed to foster emotional independence, strengthen the sense of identity, and promote healthier interaction patterns, both personally and professionally.

Recognition and Acceptance

The first step towards transformation is recognizing one's own tendencies towards codependency and unhealthy helping. This process of self-awareness involves honest and compassionate exploration of the underlying motivations behind these behaviors. Type 2 women can start by keeping a journal of their daily interactions, noting moments when they feel compelled to help and reflecting on their own emotions and needs they are trying to fulfill through these acts.

Developing Self-Awareness

Self-awareness is crucial for understanding the complexities of the type 2 personality. Meditation and mindfulness exercises can be powerful tools for cultivating mindful presence and non-judgmental observation of one's thoughts and emotions. These practices help type 2 women focus on the present moment, reducing the tendency to anticipate others' needs or seek external validation.

Establishing Healthy Boundaries

Setting clear boundaries is essential for overcoming codependency. This includes learning to say "no" assertively and without guilt, recognizing that self-care is not an act of selfishness but a fundamental need. Practical exercises, such as role-playing or scripting for difficult situations, can prepare type 2 women to implement these boundaries effectively in real life.

Fostering Emotional Independence

Emotional independence is cultivated by strengthening the relationship with oneself. This may involve dedicating time to activities and hobbies that nurture the spirit and reinforce self-esteem, regardless of others' approval. Creating a "bank of personal affirmations" with self-supporting messages and reminders of one's strengths and achievements can be a revitalizing exercise for moments of doubt or insecurity.

Celebrating Authenticity

Last but not least, it is crucial for type 2 women to embrace and celebrate their authenticity. This means valuing their own needs, desires, and emotions as much as they value others'. Participating in support groups or workshops focused on personal development can provide a safe space to share experiences and learn from others, reinforcing the importance of authenticity on the journey towards self-love and growth.

type 2 women can begin to unravel patterns of codependency and unhealthy helping, paving the way for a more loving and equitable relationship with themselves and others. This chapter not only offers practical tools for change but also invites deep reflection on the power of self-love as a source of personal growth and transformation.

The Power of Authenticity: Developing a strong sense of self-worth and personal boundaries.

In the journey of personal development and self-discovery, Enneagram Type 2 women often confront the challenge of recognizing and asserting their inherent value beyond their natural inclination to nurture and support others. This section delves into the transformative power of authenticity, a cornerstone in developing a robust sense of self-worth and establishing firm personal boundaries.

Understanding Authenticity

Authenticity emerges as a beacon of integrity and truth in the quest for personal identity and self-acceptance. For Enneagram Type 2 women, this means embracing their genuine selves, with all their strengths and vulnerabilities, independent of their roles as caretakers and supporters. This authenticity is not merely about honesty with others but, fundamentally, about being truthful with oneself.

Cultivating Self-Worth

Self-worth is the bedrock upon which authenticity stands. For Type 2s, cultivating self-worth involves a conscious shift from seeking validation through acts of service to recognizing their intrinsic value. This transformation begins with self-reflection and acknowledgment of personal needs, desires, and accomplishments. Affirmation practices, journaling, and mindfulness exercises can serve as practical tools to reinforce the belief in one's own worth, independent of external approval or acknowledgment.

Establishing Personal Boundaries

Personal boundaries are essential for protecting one's emotional and mental well-being. For Type 2 women, who are predisposed to blur these lines in their eagerness to help, learning to set and maintain boundaries is crucial. This process includes understanding one's limits, communicating them clearly to others, and honoring these limits, even when it feels uncomfortable. Role-playing scenarios and assertiveness training can empower Type 2s to express their needs and boundaries confidently, fostering healthier relationships both personally and professionally.

The Role of Vulnerability

Vulnerability is a strength that underpins authenticity. For Type 2 women, allowing themselves to be vulnerable means acknowledging that they do not always have to be the caregiver or the one who "has it all together." It involves opening up about their struggles, asking for help when needed, and accepting that imperfection is a part of being human. Embracing vulnerability can lead to deeper connections with others and a more compassionate relationship with oneself.

The Journey Towards Authentic Living

Living authentically is a dynamic and ongoing journey. It requires continuous self-awareness, the courage to face one's fears and insecurities, and the resilience to stay true to oneself in the face of external pressures to conform. For Enneagram Type 2 women, this journey towards authenticity not only fosters a strong sense of self-worth and personal boundaries but also unlocks a deeper level of personal growth and fulfillment.

The power of authenticity lies in its ability to transform the way Enneagram Type 2 women view themselves and interact with the world. By developing a strong sense of self-worth and establishing personal boundaries, Type 2s can navigate the complexities of their relationships and personal aspirations with greater confidence and clarity. This chapter has explored the pathways through which Type 2 women can embrace their authentic selves, marking a pivotal step in their journey towards self-love and growth. Through embracing authenticity, they not only enrich their own lives but also inspire those around them to embark on their own journeys of self-discovery and personal development.

Chapter 4:
Nurturing Your Wellbeing

Nourishing Body and Mind: Exploring how mindful eating habits and self-care practices can support physical and emotional wellbeing for 2s.

In a world that often demands constant giving and nurturing from others, Type 2s on the Enneagram can find themselves deprioritizing their own physical and emotional needs. This chapter delves into the crucial practice of nurturing wellbeing through mindful eating habits and self-care practices, essential for Type 2s to replenish their energy and maintain their capacity to care for others.

Understanding Mindful Eating

Mindful eating is not merely a diet or a regimen; it is a profound way of connecting with food and the act of eating, with awareness and gratitude. For Type 2s, who may sometimes use food as a source of comfort or neglect their dietary needs in the hustle of caring for others, mindful eating encourages a nurturing relationship with food that respects the body's needs. This practice involves eating slowly, savoring each bite, and listening to the body's hunger and fullness cues, fostering a healthier relationship with food and body image.

Incorporating Self-Care Practices

Self-care encompasses a wide range of practices that nourish the mind, body, and soul. For Type 2s, establishing a self-care routine is a powerful affirmation of their worth and an essential component of wellbeing. This can include regular physical activities that they enjoy, such as yoga, walking, or dancing, which help in reducing stress and increasing physical health. Equally important are practices that support mental and emotional health, such as meditation, journaling, or engaging in hobbies that bring joy and fulfillment.

The Importance of Rest and Sleep

Often overlooked but vitally important, adequate rest and sleep are foundational to physical and emotional wellbeing. Type 2s, always ready to meet the needs of others, might find it challenging to give themselves permission to rest. Prioritizing sleep and integrating relaxation techniques into the evening routine can significantly improve overall health, mood, and resilience.

Setting Boundaries for Self-Care

One of the most challenging aspects for Type 2s in nurturing their wellbeing is setting boundaries that allow for self-care. This involves learning to say no to others when necessary, recognizing that self-care is not selfish but essential for maintaining their ability to care for others effectively. Setting these boundaries can be empowering for Type 2s, as it reinforces their self-worth and commitment to their wellbeing.

Community and Connection

While self-care is an individual practice, building a supportive community can greatly enhance wellbeing. For Type 2s, who thrive on connection, finding or creating a community that supports and values self-care can provide encouragement and accountability. Whether it's a group dedicated to physical activities, a book club, or a meditation circle, being part of a community fosters a sense of belonging and support that is crucial for sustaining wellbeing practices.

the journey to nurturing their wellbeing through mindful eating and self-care practices is both a challenge and an opportunity for growth. By embracing these practices, they can create a more balanced and fulfilling life, one that honors their needs as much as they honor the needs of others. This chapter has outlined the importance of nourishing both body and mind, establishing restorative self-care routines, and the transformative power of setting boundaries for self-care. In doing so, Type 2s can ensure they have the energy, health, and vitality needed to live their lives to the fullest, enriching not only their own lives but also the lives of those they care so deeply about.

The Power of Connection and Movement: Discussing different forms of physical activity and social connection that can benefit 2s in managing stress and promoting well-being.

In the continuum of self-care and personal growth, Enneagram Type 2 women face the unique challenge of balancing their innate desire to connect and care for others with the equally important need to tend to their own well-being. This chapter explores the symbiotic relationship between physical activity and social connection as vital components of stress management and overall wellness for Type 2s.

Embracing Physical Movement

Physical activity, in its myriad forms, offers more than just physical health benefits; it is a potent stress reliever and a conduit for emotional and psychological well-being. For Type 2s, who often prioritize the needs of others above their own, incorporating regular physical movement into their routine can serve as a powerful act of self-love and self-care.

Yoga and Pilates: These practices not only improve flexibility and strength but also incorporate breathwork and mindfulness, offering a holistic approach to stress management. The emphasis on being present in the moment can help Type 2s cultivate a deeper connection to their inner selves, away from their caregiving tendencies.

Group Fitness Classes: Participating in group fitness, such as dance, aerobics, or spinning classes, combines the benefits of physical exercise with the joy of social interaction. For Type 2s, these settings provide an opportunity to engage in self-care while still fulfilling their need for connection and community.

Nature Walks and Hiking: Engaging with the natural world through walking or hiking can be incredibly therapeutic. It offers a sense of peace and grounding, reminding Type 2s of the beauty and serenity that can be found outside of their obligations to others.

Cultivating Social Connections

The health benefits of robust social connections are well-documented, including lower rates of anxiety and depression, higher self-esteem, and even a longer lifespan. For Type 2s, whose sense of purpose is often intertwined with their relationships, nurturing meaningful connections is crucial for their emotional and mental health.

Volunteering: Engaging in volunteer work allows Type 2s to fulfill their desire to help others in a structured way that respects their boundaries and personal well-being. It provides a sense of purpose and community, while also offering the chance to meet like-minded individuals.

Support Groups and Clubs: Joining support groups or clubs centered around hobbies or interests can provide a space for Type 2s to express themselves and share experiences in a supportive environment. This can foster a sense of belonging and mutual understanding.

Mindful Socializing: Encouraging Type 2s to engage in social activities that truly nourish their souls, such as intimate gatherings with close friends or family, can reinforce the quality over quantity in relationships. It's important for them to recognize the value in connections that replenish rather than deplete their emotional reserves.

For Enneagram Type 2 women, the journey towards nurturing their well-being is enriched by the integration of movement and connection into their daily lives. By embracing forms of physical activity that resonate with their personal preferences and cultivating social connections that support their emotional health, Type 2s can create a balanced and fulfilling life. This chapter has highlighted the power of these elements in managing stress and promoting overall well-being, inviting Type 2s to prioritize their health as passionately as they do the care of others. In doing so, they not only enhance their capacity for self-love but also amplify their ability to positively impact the lives of those around them, embodying the true essence of their giving nature.

Chapter 5:
Supportive Parenting

Raising Confident Children: Moving Beyond Perfectionism: Strategies for balancing expectations and fostering a positive learning environment for your children.

In the landscape of parenting, Enneagram Type 2 women are often guided by a profound sense of care, compassion, and a desire for their children to succeed. This noble intention, however, can sometimes lead to a perfectionist approach that may inadvertently pressure both the parent and child. This chapter explores strategies for moving beyond perfectionism, aiming to balance expectations and cultivate a nurturing and positive learning environment that fosters confidence and growth in children.

Understanding the Impact of Perfectionism

Perfectionism, in the context of parenting, can manifest as an overriding desire to ensure that children do not face failure or hardship. While this comes from a place of love, it can restrict children's opportunities to learn from mistakes, explore their interests freely, and develop resilience. Recognizing the subtle ways in which perfectionism can surface is the first step for Type 2 parents in adopting a more balanced approach to parenting.

Encouraging Mistakes and Learning

One of the most valuable lessons a parent can impart is that mistakes are not failures, but opportunities for learning and growth. Encouraging children to try new things, even if they might not excel at them immediately, helps to instill a growth mindset. Parents can model this behavior by sharing their own learning experiences and reactions to setbacks, thereby normalizing the process of learning through trial and error.

Fostering Autonomy and Independence

For Type 2 parents, the impulse to nurture and assist can sometimes overshadow the child's need for autonomy. Encouraging independence does not mean withdrawing support but rather providing a safe space for children to make their own decisions and solve problems. This can be as simple as allowing them to choose their own extracurricular activities or manage their homework schedule, with the understanding that the parent is always there to guide, not to dictate.

Cultivating Emotional Intelligence

Emotional intelligence is as crucial as academic success in a child's development. Type 2 parents, with their innate empathy and emotional awareness, are uniquely positioned to teach their children about emotions, empathy, and communication. Regular, open conversations about feelings, active listening, and teaching by example can help children understand and manage their emotions effectively, fostering emotional resilience and empathy towards others.

Celebrating Effort Over Achievement

Shifting the focus from outcomes to the effort and dedication put into tasks can help mitigate the effects of perfectionism. Celebrating the hard work and perseverance children show, regardless of the outcome, reinforces the value of effort and the personal growth that comes from it. This approach encourages children to value their own progress and journey, rather than just the destination or external validation.

Type 2 women, moving beyond perfectionism in parenting involves a delicate balance between offering support and allowing children the freedom to explore, make mistakes, and grow independently. By embracing strategies that prioritize learning, autonomy, emotional intelligence, and the celebration of effort, Type 2 parents can foster an environment that nurtures confident, resilient, and well-rounded individuals. This chapter not only offers practical guidance for adopting a more balanced parenting approach but also affirms the profound impact of nurturing a child's inner strength and confidence, setting the foundation for a lifetime of growth and self-discovery.

The Gift of Presence: Techniques for being present and consciously involved in parenting while also taking care of yourself.

In the demanding journey of parenting, being truly present for your children is both a gift and a challenge, especially for Enneagram Type 2 women, who are naturally inclined to nurture and support others, often at the expense of their own well-being. This chapter offers techniques for Type 2 mothers to cultivate presence and mindfulness in their parenting practices, ensuring they can offer the best of themselves to their children while also honoring their need for self-care.

Understanding the Importance of Presence

Presence in parenting means being fully engaged and attentive to your child's needs, emotions, and experiences, without distraction. For Type 2s, this requires a delicate balance between their inherent desire to provide support and the necessity of maintaining their own emotional and physical health. Being present not only strengthens the bond with your child but also models healthy emotional regulation and mindfulness.

Techniques for Cultivating Presence

Mindful Listening: Practice active listening when engaging with your children. This means putting aside your thoughts and judgments to truly hear and understand what they are expressing. Mindful listening demonstrates to your children that they are valued and respected, fostering a deeper connection.

Quality Time: Dedicate uninterrupted time with your children, where your full attention is on sharing experiences, conversations, or simply enjoying each other's company. Whether it's a short daily activity or a weekly special outing, the focus is on quality, not quantity.

Self-awareness and Regulation: Being present requires self-awareness and the ability to regulate your own emotions and responses. Techniques such as deep breathing, meditation, or even brief timeouts for yourself can help manage stress and stay centered, enabling you to respond to your children more calmly and effectively.

Setting Boundaries: Establishing clear boundaries between work, personal time, and family time can help in being more present. This includes setting aside specific times when you are fully available to your children, free from the distractions of work or other commitments.

Balancing Parenting with Self-Care

For Type 2 mothers, self-care is not selfish but essential. Taking care of yourself ensures you have the energy, patience, and emotional capacity to be fully present and supportive of your children.

Prioritize Your Well-being: Incorporate activities that replenish your energy and bring you joy into your daily routine. Whether it's exercise, reading, or a hobby, these activities are vital for maintaining your mental and physical health.

Seek Support: Acknowledge that seeking help, whether from a partner, family, friends, or professional services, is a strength. Sharing responsibilities can provide you with the necessary time to recharge and maintain your well-being.

Mindfulness Practices: Engage in mindfulness practices such as meditation, yoga, or journaling. These practices enhance your ability to stay present, both with your children and in managing your own needs and emotions.

Type 2 women, the art of being present in parenting while also taking care of themselves is a journey of constant learning and adaptation. By employing these techniques, Type 2 mothers can ensure they provide a nurturing, attentive, and emotionally rich environment for their children, built on the foundation of a healthy and balanced approach to their own well-being. This chapter has explored how the gift of presence enriches the parenting experience, fostering deeper connections and promoting growth and resilience in both children and parents.

Chapter 6:
Exploring Your Spiritual Path

The Enneagram and Your Deepest Longing: Exploring how the Enneagram can be a tool for deepening spiritual connection for 2s.
In the quest for self-discovery and spiritual growth, the Enneagram serves as a map that guides individuals through the complex landscape of their inner world. For Enneagram Type 2 women, this journey involves exploring the depths of their deepest longings – for love, connection, and recognition – and how these desires shape their spiritual path. This chapter delves into how the Enneagram, as an ancient tool of wisdom, can facilitate a deeper spiritual connection by revealing the motivations, fears, and potential for growth inherent in Type 2s.

Understanding the Spiritual Essence of Type 2s

At their core, Type 2s are driven by a desire to be loved and appreciated for who they are, often manifesting through acts of service and nurturing towards others. However, this outward focus can sometimes lead them away from attending to their own spiritual needs and inner growth. The Enneagram illuminates this pattern, inviting Type 2s to embark on a spiritual journey towards self-love and acceptance, recognizing that true fulfillment comes from within, not from external validation.

The Role of the Enneagram in Spiritual Development

Self-Awareness: The Enneagram shines a light on the habits of thought, emotion, and behavior that can hinder spiritual growth. For Type 2s, becoming aware of their tendency to seek love by serving others at the expense of their well-being is the first step towards spiritual transformation.

Moving Beyond the Ego: The Enneagram encourages individuals to explore beyond their egoic identity, offering a pathway to discover the essence of their true self. For Type 2s, this means learning to value themselves independently of their helpfulness to others, and finding a source of unconditional love within.

Cultivating Inner Balance: By understanding their Enneagram type, Type 2s can work towards balancing their innate generosity with self-care and boundary setting. This inner balance is crucial for spiritual growth, as it allows for a harmonious relationship with oneself and the Divine.

Deepening Compassion: The journey through the Enneagram fosters a deep compassion for oneself and others. Type 2s, who naturally empathize with others, are invited to extend this compassion inwards, healing the parts of themselves that feel unworthy of love unless they are giving.

Practical Spiritual Practices for Type 2s

Mindfulness and Meditation: Engaging in mindfulness and meditation can help Type 2s to center themselves and connect with their inner spirituality, reducing the compulsion to constantly seek approval through actions.

Journaling for Self-Reflection: Regular journaling offers Type 2s a private space for self-reflection and dialogue with their inner selves, facilitating a deeper understanding of their spiritual longings and how they can fulfill them independently.

Spiritual Community: Participating in a spiritual community provides Type 2s with a sense of belonging and connection, while also offering perspectives that challenge them to grow beyond their comfort zones.

Service as a Path to Self-Discovery: When approached mindfully, service can be a path to spiritual growth for Type 2s. Engaging in volunteer work with the intention of self-discovery rather than validation can be a powerful practice of love in action.

Spiritual Practices for Nurturing the Soul: Incorporating a variety of spiritual practices that may resonate with different readers, such as meditation, nature connection, or service to others.

The spiritual journey is deeply personal and unique to each individual, yet the ancient wisdom of the Enneagram provides a universal map for exploration and growth. For Enneagram Type 2 women, nurturing the soul through varied spiritual practices offers a pathway to balance their innate desire to give with the equally important need for self-replenishment and inner peace. This chapter explores a spectrum of spiritual practices that can enrich the spiritual life of Type 2s, supporting their journey towards self-discovery, inner tranquility, and a more profound connection with the world around them.

Meditation and Mindfulness

Meditation and mindfulness practices stand as pillars of spiritual growth, offering a sanctuary of peace in the bustling world. For Type 2s, these practices can be particularly transformative, providing a space for introspection, self-acceptance, and the cultivation of inner silence. Whether through guided meditations, mindfulness breathing exercises, or silent contemplation, these practices help to quiet the mind, allowing Type 2s to connect with their deeper selves beyond the roles they play in the lives of others.

Nature Connection

The natural world offers a powerful source of spiritual nourishment and grounding. For Type 2s, spending time in nature—whether walking in a forest, gardening, or simply sitting by a stream—can be a profound practice of reconnection to the Earth's inherent wisdom and beauty. These moments of nature connection foster a sense of belonging to something greater than oneself, providing perspective, inspiration, and a deep sense of calm.

Service to Others

Service, when approached as a spiritual practice, can be a path of profound growth and fulfillment for Type 2s. Engaging in service with mindfulness and intention transforms the act of giving into a practice of love in action, offering opportunities for self-transcendence and the realization of interconnectedness with others. Volunteering for causes that resonate deeply, participating in community service, or simply offering acts of kindness in daily life can become meaningful expressions of Type 2s' spiritual values.

Journaling and Reflective Writing

Journaling and reflective writing offer powerful tools for self-exploration and spiritual reflection. For Type 2s, keeping a spiritual journal can be a valuable practice for processing emotions, exploring inner conflicts, and documenting insights gained through other spiritual practices. Writing can serve as a form of meditation, a way to communicate with one's higher self, and a means to recognize and appreciate the journey of growth and transformation.

Yoga and Physical Movement

Yoga and other forms of intentional physical movement can be deeply spiritual practices that unite body, mind, and spirit. For Type 2s, engaging in yoga, tai chi, qigong, or even dance can provide a means of expressing and experiencing spirituality through the physical body. These practices offer a way to release stored emotions, increase mindfulness, and cultivate a sense of harmony and balance within oneself.

Exploring a spiritual path is a journey of discovery, growth, and deepening connection with oneself and the world. For Enneagram Type 2 women, incorporating a variety of spiritual practices into their lives offers a rich tapestry of experiences that nurture the soul, balance their giving nature with receiving, and promote a profound sense of well-being. This chapter has highlighted several practices that can support Type 2s in their spiritual exploration, inviting them to embrace their journey with curiosity, compassion, and an open heart. By engaging in these practices, Type 2s can cultivate a deeper, more fulfilling spiritual life, enriching their experience of themselves and their capacity to give and receive love.

Chapter 7:
Growth and Integration

Your Wings: Understanding the Influences of Type Three and Type One

The wings of the Enneagram offer profound insights into the nuanced dimensions of personality, enriching our understanding of ourselves and how we interact with the world. For Enneagram Type 2 women, the adjacent types—Type 3 (The Achiever) and Type 1 (The Perfectionist)—serve as wings that influence their core type in significant ways. This section delves into how these wings, Type 2w3 and Type 2w1, color their personalities, preferences, and challenges, contributing to a richer tapestry of self-understanding and growth.

Type 2w3: The Host/Hostess

Type 2s with a Three wing (2w3) blend the warmth, generosity, and people-oriented nature of Type 2 with the ambition, efficiency, and charisma of Type 3. This combination creates individuals who are particularly attuned to the value of relationships in achieving success and recognition. They are often seen as charming, engaging, and adept at navigating social situations, using their understanding of emotions to foster connections that further their goals and the goals of those they care for.

Characteristics of 2w3:

Ambitious Altruism: 2w3s harness their ambition not just for personal gain but as a means to assist and uplift others. They are often involved in community work, social causes, or roles that allow them to use their influence for the betterment of society.

Adaptive Social Skills: With a natural charisma, 2w3s excel in social situations, easily adapting their approach to fit the mood and needs of those around them. They have a keen sense of how to present themselves in the best light to be both likable and effective.

Challenges: The main challenge for 2w3s lies in balancing their need for achievement with their genuine desire to help others. They may struggle with issues of authenticity, sometimes wondering if their actions are motivated by selfless love or the desire for accolades.

Type 2w1: The Servant

Type 2s with a One wing (2w1) merge the loving, other-focused nature of Type 2 with the integrity, ethical standards, and self-discipline of Type 1. This blend creates individuals who are deeply committed to improving the world around them through service and adherence to high moral standards. They approach their supportive roles with a sense of duty, often taking on responsibilities that others might overlook.

Characteristics of 2w1:

Principled Caregiving: 2w1s offer their support and care not just out of empathy, but as part of a moral or ethical obligation. They are driven by a vision of how things "should be," applying this vision to their efforts to help and uplift others.

Attention to Detail: With their One wing, 2w1s bring a meticulous attention to detail in their endeavors. They are thorough in their assistance, ensuring that their help meets not only the immediate needs but also aligns with a larger framework of improvement.

Challenges: The challenge for 2w1s lies in their inner critic, which can amplify feelings of guilt or inadequacy when they fall short of their own or others' expectations. They must navigate the delicate balance between self-improvement and self-acceptance, learning to appreciate their efforts without being overly harsh on themselves.

Growth and Integration for 2w3 and 2w1

For both 2w3s and 2w1s, growth involves embracing the strengths of their wings while addressing the challenges they bring. 2w3s can strive for authenticity in their achievements and relationships, recognizing that their value does not depend on external validation. Meanwhile, 2w1s can learn to soften their self-criticism and appreciate the beauty in imperfection, understanding that true service comes from a place of love, not obligation.

In integrating the positive aspects of their wings, Type 2 women can embark on a journey of profound personal development, enhancing their capacity to love, serve, and achieve with authenticity and grace. This chapter not only illuminates the complex interplay between Type 2 and its wings but also offers a roadmap for leveraging these influences towards greater self-awareness, fulfillment, and impact.

Growth and Integration: Moving Towards Health

For Enneagram Type 2 women, the journey of growth and integration involves a dynamic interplay between moving towards the healthy aspects of Type Four in times of growth, and managing the stress-induced movement towards Type Eight. This chapter examines these paths of integration and disintegration, providing insights and strategies for Type 2s to navigate these transitions with awareness and grace, ultimately leading to a more balanced and fulfilling life.

Understanding Integration Towards Type Four

In their growth path, Type 2s move towards the positive attributes of Type Four, embracing deeper levels of self-awareness, authenticity, and emotional depth. This movement encourages Type 2s to explore their inner landscapes, acknowledge their true feelings, and express their individuality. Rather than seeking validation through helping others, Type 2s learn to appreciate their intrinsic worth, cultivating a rich inner world where they can find creativity, inspiration, and a sense of uniqueness.

Strategies for Integration Towards Type Four:

Embrace Authenticity: Encourage self-reflection to discover personal desires and values beyond the role of the caregiver. Journaling, artistic expression, and therapy can be valuable tools for this exploration.

Acknowledge and Express Emotions: Allow yourself to feel and express a range of emotions without judgment. Practice identifying and communicating your feelings in a healthy way.

Cultivate Creativity: Engage in creative activities for the sake of self-expression, not for external approval. This could include painting, writing, music, or any form of art that resonates with you.

Managing Disintegration Towards Type Eight

Under stress, Type 2s may exhibit characteristics of Type Eight, displaying assertiveness that can verge on aggression, a need to control their environment, and a struggle with vulnerability. Recognizing these stress-induced behaviors is crucial for Type 2s to maintain their emotional balance and nurture their relationships.

Strategies for Managing Movement Towards Type Eight:

Recognize Stress Signals: Become aware of the early signs of moving towards Type Eight, such as increased irritability or a desire to dominate situations.

Practice Mindfulness: Use mindfulness and relaxation techniques to manage stress and avoid reactive behaviors. Deep breathing, meditation, and yoga can help regain a sense of calm.

Seek Constructive Outlets: Channel the intensity into constructive activities, such as physical exercise or engaging in passionate projects that align with your values.

Integration for Balanced Living

The journey of growth for Enneagram Type 2 women involves a delicate balance between embracing the depth and authenticity of Type Four and managing the assertive qualities of Type Eight. By understanding these dynamics, Type 2s can navigate their path with greater self-awareness and intentionality.

Exploring the pathways of integration and disintegration provides Enneagram Type 2 women with a roadmap for personal growth and emotional resilience. Embracing the emotional depth of Type Four allows for a richer, more authentic experience of life, while effectively managing the movement towards Type Eight ensures that stress does not overshadow their inherent warmth and compassion. This chapter has offered insights and practical strategies for Type 2s to cultivate a balanced and fulfilling journey of self-discovery, integration, and growth, marking significant steps towards a healthy, integrated life that honors both their needs and the gifts they offer to the world.

CHAPTER 8

WORKBOOK

Did you love *The woman of enneagram 2*? Then you should read *The woman of Enneagram 1: Love Marriage Success Edition*[1] by Maria Rondon!

Enneagram Type 1 Woman: Unleash Your Inner Perfection (Enneagram Book, Enneagram for Adult Women)

Discover the transformative power of the Enneagram as a Type 1 woman. This life-changing book provides invaluable insights into the core motivations, strengths, and growth opportunities for the Perfectionist personality type.

As an Enneagram Type 1, you strive for excellence, order, and integrity in all aspects of life. While these qualities are admirable, they can also lead to self-criticism, rigid thinking, and a fear of making

---

1. https://books2read.com/u/mvMrye

2. https://books2read.com/u/mvMrye

mistakes. This book empowers you to embrace your true essence while breaking free from limiting patterns.

Through thought-provoking exercises and real-life examples, you'll explore how the Enneagram impacts your relationships (Enneagram in Love, Enneagram in Marriage), career, and personal growth journey. Gain a deeper understanding of your drives, learn to temper your inner critic, and develop self-compassion and balance.

Whether you're seeking to improve your relationships, advance in your career, or simply live a more authentic and fulfilling life, this book is a powerful guide. It offers practical strategies and insights to help you harness the strengths of your Type 1 personality while addressing your core fears and blind spots.

Dive into this life-changing book today and embark on a journey of self-discovery, personal empowerment (Enneagram Empowerment), and profound growth (Enneagram for Personal Growth). Unlock your true potential as an Enneagram Type 1 woman and live with greater presence, purpose, and inner peace.

Also by Maria Rondon

Alzheimer
Alzheimer Guia para cuidadores

Enneagram For Women
The woman of Enneagram 1: Love Marriage Success Edition
The woman of enneagram 2
The woman of Enneagram 3: Love marriage success edition
The Woman of Enneagram 4: Love, Marriage, Success Edition
The woman of Enneagram 5: Love marriage success edition
The Woman of Enneagram 6: Love, Marriage, Success Edition
The woman of Enneagram 7: Love marriage success edition
The woman of Enneagram 8: Love marriage success edition
The woman of Enneagram 9: Love marriage success edition

LOA
El secreto para atraer tu alma gemela

www.ingramcontent.com/pod-product-compliance
Lightning Source LLC
Chambersburg PA
CBHW021753150726
47989CB00004B/1639